THE BEST OF BROADWAY

Complete Words and Music

80 GREAT SONGS OF THE AMERICAN MUSICAL THEATRE

arranged for PIANO, VOCAL and GUITAR

FOR THE 83 SONGS USED IN THIS BOOK, GRATEFUL ACKNOWLEDGEMENTS TO:

Belwin-Mills Publishing Corp. — Ain't Misbehavin', Corner Of The Sky, I Can't Give You Anything But Love, It Don't Mean A Thing, Magic To Do, Mood Indigo, Solitude, Sophisticated Lady, When You And I Were Young Maggie Blues.

Harrison Music Corp. — Do Nothin' Till You Hear From Me, Don't Get Around Much Anymore.

Gus Kahn Music Co. — Makin' Whoopee!

Livingston and Evans, Inc. — Sugar Baby Bounce.

Tempo Music, Inc. — Perdido, Satin Doll, Take The 'A' Train.

The Times Square Music Publications Co. — Fiddler On The Roof, If I Were A Rich Man, Matchmaker, Sunrise Sunset.

Edwin H. Morris & Company, *A division of MPL Communications, Inc.* — The remaining 63 songs.

7126

THE BEST OF BROADWAY

80 Great Songs of the American Musical Theatre

THE BEST OF BROADWAY

80 Great Songs of the American Musical Theatre

From the Broadway Musical "A Chorus Line"

What I Did For Love

Lyrics and Music by
Marvin Hamlisch, Edward Kleban

From the Broadway Musical "A Chorus Line"

One

Lyrics and Music by
Marvin Hamlisch, Edward Kleban

From the Broadway Musical "Shenandoah"

Freedom

Lyrics and Music by
Peter Udell, Gary Geld

AIN'T MISBEHAVIN'

Words by ANDY RAZAF   Music by THOMAS "FATS" WALLER and HARRY BROOKS

From the Broadway Musical "Ain't Misbehavin'"

Ain't Misbehavin'

Lyrics and Music by Andy Razaf,
Thomas "Fats" Waller, Harry Brooks

From the Broadway Musical "Ain't Misbehavin' "

Alligator Crawl

Lyrics and Music by
Thomas "Fats" Waller

From the Broadway Musical "Ain't Misbehavin' "

Vipers' Drag

Lyrics and Music by
Thomas "Fats" Waller

From the Broadway Musical "Ain't Misbehavin'"

I'm Gonna Sit Right Down And Write Myself A Letter

Lyrics and Music by
Joe Young, Fred E. Ahlert

Refrain

a tempo (with a lilt)

I'm Gon-na Sit Right Down And Write My-self A Let - ter____ And make be-lieve it came from you._____ I'm gon-na write words, oh, so sweet, They're gon-na knock me off my feet. A lot of kiss-es on the bot-tom, I'll be glad I got 'em,____ I'm gon-na

From the Broadway Musical "Annie"

Easy Street

Lyrics and Music by
Martin Charnin, Charles Strouse

From the Broadway Musical "Annie"

Tomorrow

Lyrics and Music by
Martin Charnin, Charles Strouse

From the Broadway Musical "Annie"

You're Never Fully Dressed Without A Smile

Lyrics and Music by
Martin Charnin, Charles Strouse

From the Broadway Musical "Annie"

Maybe

Lyrics and Music by
Martin Charnin, Charles Strouse

From the Musical "Bye Bye Birdie"

Bye Bye Birdie

Lyrics and Music by
Lee Adams, Charles Strouse

From the Broadway Musical "Bye Bye Birdie"

Kids!

Lyrics and Music by
Lee Adams, Charles Strouse

From the Broadway Musical "Bye Bye Birdie"

A Lot Of Livin' To Do

Lyrics and Music by
Lee Adams, Charles Strouse

From the Broadway Musical "Bye Bye Birdie"

Put On A Happy Face

Lyrics and Music by
Lee Adams, Charles Strouse

From the Broadway Musical "A Chorus Line"

At The Ballet

Lyrics and Music by
Marvin Hamlisch, Edward Kleban

From the Broadway Musical "A Chorus Line"

Dance: Ten; Looks: Three

Lyrics and Music by
Marvin Hamlisch, Edward Kleban

From the Broadway Musical "A Chorus Line"

Hello Twelve, Hello Thirteen, Hello Love

Lyrics and Music by
Marvin Hamlisch, Edward Kleban

Happy, bright Rock

From the Broadway Musical "A Chorus Line"

I Can Do That

Lyrics and Music by
Marvin Hamlisch, Edward Kleban

From the Broadway Musical "Damn Yankees"

Heart

Lyrics and Music by
Richard Adler, Jerry Ross

From the Broadway Musical "Damn Yankees"

Whatever Lola Wants (Lola Gets)

Lyrics and Music by
Richard Adler, Jerry Ross

1127

83

From the Broadway Musical "Dear World"

Dear World

Music and Lyric by
Jerry Herman

With dignity

1. Please take your med - i - cine,
2. Please keep your fe - ver down,   } DEAR   WORLD,
3. Some - one has wound - ed you,

Please keep your pres - sure down,
Please keep your cour - age up,   } DEAR   WORLD.
Some - one has poi - soned you,

Prom - ise to thrive___ on each word your doc - tor speaks,
Your vim and vig - or is ve - ry sore - ly missed,
And those who love___ you de - fi - ant - ly in - sist

From the Broadway Musical "Drat! The Cat!"

I Like Him

Lyrics and Music by
Ira Levin, Milton Schafer

From the Broadway Musical "Drat! The Cat!"

She Touched Me

Lyrics and Music by
Ira Levin, Milton Schafer

From the Broadway Musical "Fiddler On The Roof"

Fiddler On The Roof

Lyrics and Music by
Sheldon Harnick, Jerry Bock

Tevye (TOPOL) and Golde (NORMA CRANE) sing "Do You Love Me?"

Tevye (TOPOL), gives his blessing to his daughter, Hodel (MICHELE MARSH) and Perchik (MICHAEL GLASER) with permission to marry.

Tevye's five daughters sing "Matchmaker, Matchmaker." From left to right are Chava (NEVA SMALL), Bielka (CANDICE BONSTEIN), Tzeitel (ROSALIND HARRIS), Shprintze (ELAINE EDWARDS) and Hodel (MICHELE MARSH).

Tevye (TOPOL) sings "IF I WERE A RICH MAN"

Hodel (MICHELE MARSH) and Perchik (MICHAEL GLASER) break with tradition and dance together.

Motel (LEONARD FREY) sings "Miracle of Miracles" to his betrother, Tzeitel (ROSALIND HARRIS).

43893

From the Broadway Musical "Fiddler On The Roof"

If I Were A Rich Man

Lyrics and Music by
Sheldon Harnick, Jerry Bock

Reflective, lyrical, soft

know.   If I were rich I'd have the time that I lack. To

sit in the syn-a-gogue and pray;   And may-be have a   seat by the east-ern wall.

And I'd dis - cuss the ho - ly   books with the learn-ed men sev-en ho-urs ev-'ry

day;   This would be the   sweet-est thing of   all._____ (Sigh)

From the Broadway Musical "Fiddler On The Roof"

Matchmaker

Lyrics and Music by
Sheldon Harnick, Jerry Bock

106

From the Broadway Musical "Fiddler On The Roof"

Sunrise, Sunset

Lyrics and Music by
Sheldon Harnick, Jerry Bock

From the Broadway Musical "Grease"

Freddy, My Love

Lyrics and Music by
Warren Casey, Jim Jacobs

Slow Rock tempo

1. Fred - dy, My Love, I miss you more than__ words can say,
2. (Fred - dy, you) know, your ab - sence makes me__ feel so blue;
3. (Fred - dy, you'll) see, you'll hold me in your__ arms some day;

Fred - dy, My Love, please keep in touch while__ you're a - way.
That's o - kay, though, your pre - sents make me__ think of you.
And I will be wear - ing your lace - y__ loun - je - ray,

From the Broadway Musical "Grease"

Look At Me, I'm Sandra Dee

Lyrics and Music by
Warren Casey, Jim Jacobs

Dor - is Day. I don't drink or swear, I don't

rat my hair, I get ill from one cig - ar - ette,

Keep your filth - y paws off my silk - y drawers, would you

pull that stuff with An - nette?

118

1126

REPRISE: EXTRA LYRIC

Look at me, there has to be
Something more than what they see
Wholesome and pure, also scared and unsure
A poor man's Sandra Dee.
When they criticize and make fun of me,
Can't they see the tears in my smile?
Don't they realize there's just one of me,
And it has to last me awhile.

Sandy, you must start anew,
Don't you know what you must do?
Hold your head up high, take a deep breath and cry
Goodbye
To Sandra Dee.

WE GO TOGETHER
Top: Garn Stephens.
Left to right: Timothy Meyers, Adrienne Barbeau,
Katie Hanley, Jim Borrelli, Barry Bostwick,
Marya Small, James Canning and Walter Bobbie.

From the Broadway Musical "Grease"

Summer Nights

Lyrics and Music by
Warren Casey, Jim Jacobs

126

1126

From the Broadway Musical "Guys And Dolls"

Guys And Dolls

Lyrics and Music by
Frank Loesser

From the Broadway Musical "Guys And Dolls"

Adelaide's Lament

Lyrics and Music by
Frank Loesser

134

From the Broadway Musical "Guys And Dolls"

I've Never Been In Love Before

Lyrics and Music by
Frank Loesser

From the Broadway Musical "Guys And Dolls"

Luck Be A Lady

Lyrics and Music by
Frank Loesser

yet be-fore this eve-ning is ov-er you might give me the brush.__ You

might for-get your man-ners, you might re-fuse to stay, And so the best that I can do is

Brightly

pray.__

Chorus

Luck be a la-dy to-night _____

Nev - er get out of my sight____

Stick with me ba - by I'm the fel - low you came in with,

Luck be a la - dy, luck be a la - dy, Luck be a la - dy to-night.

From the Broadway Musical "Guys And Dolls"

If I Were A Bell

Lyrics and Music by
Frank Loesser

From the Broadway Musical "Hello, Dolly!"

Hello, Dolly!

Music and Lyric by
Jerry Herman

I went a-way from the lights of Four-teenth Street And

In-to my per-son-al haze; But

now that I'm back in the lights of Four-teenth Street, To-

Refrain- Medium Strut tempo

From the Broadway Musical "Hello, Dolly!"

Before The Parade Passes By

Music and Lyric by
Jerry Herman

From the Broadway Musical "Hello, Dolly!"

It Only Takes A Moment

Music and Lyric by
Jerry Herman

Coda

long. And that is all that love's a-

bout And we'll re - call when time runs out

That it on - ly took a mo - ment

To be loved a whole life long.

From the Broadway Musical "House Of Flowers"

A Sleepin' Bee

Lyrics and Music by
Harold Arlen, Truman Capote

When you're in love and you are won-d'rin', if he real-ly is the one. There's an an-cient sign sure to tell you if your search is o-ver and done. Catch a bee and if he don't sting you, you're in a spell that's just be-gun. It's a

From the Broadway Musical "House Of Flowers"

Two Ladies In De Shade Of The Banana Tree

Lyrics and Music by
Truman Capote, Harold Arlen

street - band brings.   Fool wid fem - in - i - ni - ty   fit   fo' kings.

Dm7   G7   Am7   Ab9

Look?   See?   Nice?   A - gree?   TWO

Cm7-5   Am7-5   G9   G7-9   C6

LA-DIES IN DE SHADE OF DE BA - NA - NA   TREE._____
(Ba - nah - na)

F9

From the Broadway Musical "How To Succeed In Business Without Really Trying"

Brotherhood Of Man

With a Handclapper Spiritual Feeling

Lyrics and Music by
Frank Loesser

From the Broadway Musical "How To Succeed In Business Without Really Trying"

I Believe In You

Lyrics and Music by
Frank Loesser

From the Broadway Musical "How To Succeed In Business Without Really Trying"

Rosemary

Lyrics and Music by
Frank Loesser

Rose

Jay Pierre - pont, _____

ma - ry, } there is won-der-ful mu - sic in the ver - y

sound _____

of your name. _____

accel.

From the Broadway Musical "Kismet"

Baubles, Bangles And Beads

Lyrics and Music by
Robert Wright, George Forrest

From the Broadway Musical "Kismet"

And This Is My Beloved

*Lyrics and Music by
Robert Wright, George Forrest*

From the Broadway Musical "Kismet"

Strangers In Paradise

Lyrics and Music by
Robert Wright, George Forrest

190

fer- vent prayer___ Of a strang- er in par-a-dise? Don't send me in dark des- pair___

___ From all that I hun-ger for, But o- pen your an- gel's arms___

___ To the strang- er in par- a- dise And tell {him/her} that {he/she} need be___

___ A strang- er no more.___

1126

From the Broadway Musical "Mack And Mabel"

I Won't Send Roses

Music and Lyric by
Jerry Herman

Moderately

I won't send ros - es or hold the door;
fran - tic, my tem - per's cross;

I won't re - mem - ber which dress you wore.
With words ro - man - tic I'm at a loss.

My heart is too much in con - trol, the lack of
I'd be the first one to a - gree that I'm pre -

43893

From the Broadway Musical "Little Me"

Real Live Girl

Lyrics and Music by
Carolyn Leigh, Cy Coleman

Old-fashioned waltz tempo *(moderately bright)*

Pardon me, miss, but I've nev-er done this with a REAL LIVE
Noth-ing can beat get-ting swept off your feet by a REAL LIVE

GIRL, ___ Strayed off the farm with an ac-tu-al arm-ful of
GIRL, ___ Dreams in your bunk don't com-pare with a hunk of a

REAL LIVE GIRL. ___ Par-don me if your af-
REAL LIVE GIRL. ___ Speak-ing of mir-a-cles,

fec-tion-ate squeeze. Fogs up my gog-gles and buck-les my knees,
this must be it, Just when I start-ed to learn how to knit,

From the Broadway Musical "Mame"

Mame

Music and Lyric by
Jerry Herman

With a lilt

Chorus

1. You coax the blues right out __ of the horn, MAME,—
2. You've brought the cake-walk back __ in-to style, MAME,—

You charm the husk right off __ of the corn, MAME,—
You make the weep-in' wil-low tree smile, MAME,—

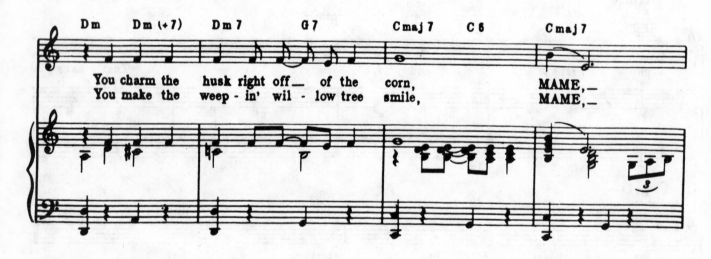

198

ANGELA LANSBURY and FRANKIE MICHAELS

From the Broadway Musical "Mame"

If He Walked Into My Life

Music and Lyric by
Jerry Herman

Verse (ad lib.)

Girl: Where's that boy with the bu - gle?
Boy: Where's that girl with the prom - ise?

The My lit - tle love who was
The girl who tried to

al - ways my big ro - mance;
show me what love could be;

Where's that boy with the bu - gle? And
Where's that girl with the prom - ise? And

why did I ev - er buy him those damn long pants?
why do I feel the some - one to blame is me?

From the Broadway Musical "Mame"

We Need A Little Christmas

Music and Lyric by
Jerry Herman

Brightly (as a polka)

1. Haul out the hol - ly,_____ Put up the
   climb down the chim - ney,_____ Turn on the

   tree be - fore my spir - it falls_____ a - gain;
   bright - est string of lights I've ev - er seen;

From the Broadway Musical "Milk And Honey"

Milk And Honey

Music and Lyric by
Jerry Herman

209

From the Broadway Musical "The Most Happy Fella"

The Most Happy Fella

Lyrics and Music by
Frank Loesser

From the Broadway Musical "The Most Happy Fella"

Standing On The Corner

Lyrics and Music by
Frank Loesser

HERMAN and BOYS:

1. Stand-ing On The Cor-er watch-ing all the girls go by,
2. Stand-ing On The Cor-er watch-ing all the girls go by,
3. Stand-ing On The Cor-er watch-ing all the girls go by,

Stand-ing On The Cor-er watch-ing all the girls go
Stand-ing On The Cor-er giv-ing all the girls the
Stand-ing On The Cor-er un-der-neath a spring-time

by Broth-er you don't know a nic-er oc-cu-
eye Broth-er if you've got a rich i-mag-i-
sky Broth-er you can't go to jail for what you're

From the Broadway Musical "The Music Man"

Till There Was You

Lyrics and Music by
Meredith Willson

Voice

There were bells on the hill, but I nev-er heard them ring-ing, No, I nev-er heard them at all Till There Was You._____ There were birds in the sky, but I

From the Broadway Musical "The Music Man"

Goodnight, My Someone

Lyrics and Music by
Meredith Willson

From the Broadway Musical "The Music Man"

Lida Rose

Lyrics and Music by
Meredith Willson

From the Broadway Musical "The Music Man"

Seventy Six Trombones

Lyrics and Music by
Meredith Willson

Thun - der - ing, thun - der - ing, loud - er than be - fore. Clar - i nets of

ev - 'ry size and trum-pet - ers who'd im - pro-vise a full oc - tave high - er than the

score.

Sev - en - ty Six Trom - bones led the big pa - rade,_____ When the or - der to

one and on-ly bass, And I oom-pahed up and down the square.____

A la Tuba

Buh buh buh buh buh buh buh buh buh buh buh,____ Buh buh buh buh buh

buh buh buh buh buh buh.____ Buh buh buh buh buh

buh buh buh buh buh buh buh buh buh buh

From the Broadway Musical "The Music Man"

Ya Got Trouble

Lyrics and Music by
Meredith Willson

240

trou-ble. That game with the fif-teen num-bered balls__ is the dev-ils tool!

Oh yes we've got trou-ble, trou-ble, trou-ble. Yes we got

trou-ble here,__ we got big, big trou-ble with a "T"

Got-ta rhyme it with "P" and that stands for pool!__

From the Broadway Musical "The Nervous Set"

The Ballad Of The Sad Young Men

Lyrics and Music by
Fran Landesman, Tommy Wolf

Sing a song of sad young men, glass-es full of rye;
Au-tumn turns the leaves to gold, slow-ly dies the heart;

All the news is bad a-gain, kiss your dreams good-bye.
Sad young men are grow-ing old, that's the cru-el-est part.

All the sad young men, sit-ting in the bars, Know-ing ne-on
All the sad young men, seek a cer-tain smile, Some-one they can

The Ballad Of The Sad Young Men - 1 of 3

The Ballad Of The Sad Young Men - 3 of 3

From the Broadway Musical "New York, New York"

Do Nothin' Till You Hear From Me

Lyrics and Music by
Bob Russell, Duke Ellington

From the Broadway Musical "New York, New York"

Don't Get Around Much Anymore

Lyric by
BOB RUSSELL

Lyrics and Music by
Duke Ellington

CHORUS Slowly
tacet

Missed the Sat-ur-day dance   Heard they crowd-ed the floor

Could-n't bear it with-out ___ you ___   Don't Get A-round Much An-y-more

tacet

Thought I'd vis-it the club   Got as far as the door

They'd have asked me a-bout ___ you ___   Don't Get A-round Much An-y-more ___

From the Broadway Musical "The Pajama Game"

Hernando's Hideaway

Lyrics and Music by
Richard Adler, Jerry Ross

But if you go to the spot that I am think-in' of,

You will be free to gaze at me and talk of

love! Just knock three times and whis-per low,

That you and I were sent by Joe, Then strike a match and

you will know, You're in Her-nan-do's Hide-a-way! O-lay!! I way! O-lay!!

From the Broadway Musical "The Pajama Game"

Small Talk

Lyrics and Music by
Richard Adler, Jerry Ross

43893

From the Broadway Musical "The Pajama Game"

Hey There

Lyrics and Music by
Richard Adler, Jerry Ross

From the Broadway Musical "Peter Pan"

I Won't Grow Up

Lyrics and Music by
Carolyn Leigh, Mark Charlap

Moderately Bright

From the Broadway Musical "Peter Pan"

I've Gotta Crow

Lyrics and Music by
Carolyn Leigh, Mark Charlap

From the Broadway Musical "Pippin"

Magic To Do

Lyrics and Music by
Stephen Schwartz

From the Broadway Musical "Pippin"

Corner Of The Sky

Lyrics and Music by
Stephen Schwartz

Ev-'ry-thing has its sea - son, ____
Ev-'ry man has his day - dreams, ____
may-be some mist - y day, ____ you'll ____

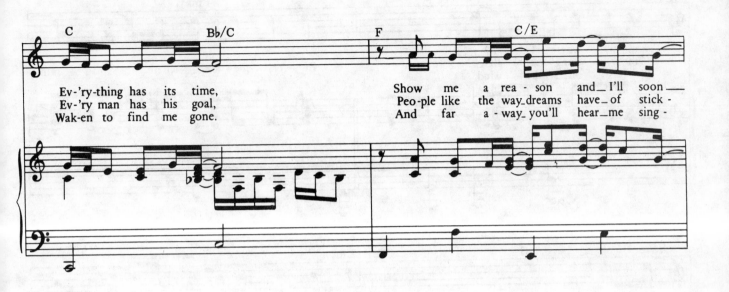

Ev-'ry-thing has its time,
Ev-'ry man has his goal,
Wak-en to find me gone.

Show me a rea - son and I'll soon
Peo-ple like the way dreams have of stick-
And far a - way you'll hear me sing-

_show you a _ rhyme.
-ing to the soul.
-ing to the dawn.

Cats fit on the win-dow sill, _
Rain comes af - ter thun - der, _
And you'll won -der if I'm hap-py there _ A

Chil -dren fit in the snow.
Win - ter comes af - ter fall.
lit - tle more than I've been.

Why do I feel I _ don't fit _ in
Some -times I think I'm not af - ter
And the an - swer will come back to _ you like laugh-

of the sky.

of the sky.

And

From the Broadway Musical "Sophisticated Ladies"

Sophisticated Lady

Lyrics and Music by
Irving Mills, Mitchell Parish, Duke Ellington

From the Broadway Musical "Sophisticated Ladies"

Mood Indigo

Lyrics and Music by
Duke Ellington, Irving Mills, Albany Bigard

From the Broadway Musical "Sophisticated Ladies"

It Don't Mean A Thing

Lyrics and Music by
Duke Ellington, Irving Mills

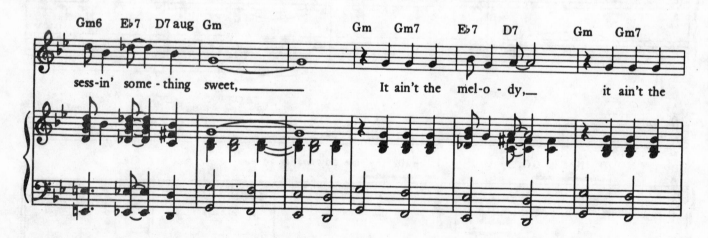

doo wah, doo wah, doo wah,) It makes no dif-f'rence if ___ it's sweet or

hot, _____ Just give that rhy-thm ev-'ry-thing you got, Oh, it

don't mean a thing, if it ain't got that swing,___ (doo wah, doo wah,

doo wah, doo wah, doo wah,___ doo wah, doo wah, doo wah.) It wah.)

From the Broadway Musical "Sophisticated Ladies"

Perdido

Lyrics and Music by
H.J. Lengsfelder, Ervin Drake, Juan Tizol

From the Broadway Musical "Sophisticated Ladies"

Satin Doll

Lyrics and Music by
Duke Ellington, Johnny Mercer, Billy Strayhorn

From the Broadway Musical "Sophisticated Ladies"

Solitude

Lyrics and Music by
Duke Ellington, Eddie DeLange, Irving Mills

Slowly, with expression

In my sol - i - tude ___ you haunt me With

re - ver - ies ___ of days gone by ___ In my sol - i - tude ___ you

taunt me With mem - o - ries ___ that nev - er die ___ I

V 226

From the Broadway Musical "Sophisticated Ladies"

Take The "A" Train

Lyrics and Music by
Billy Strayhorn, The Delta Rhythm Boys

You _____ must TAKE THE "A" TRAIN _____

To _____ go to Sug-ar Hill 'way up in Har-lem. _____

If _____ you miss the "A" train, _____ You'll

find you've missed the quick-est way to Har-lem _____ Hur-ry, —

From the Broadway Musical "Sugar Babies"

I Can't Give You Anything But Love

Lyrics and Music by
Dorothy Fields, Jimmy McHugh

From the Broadway Musical "Sugar Babies"

Sugar Baby Bounce

Lyrics and Music by
Jay Livingston, Ray Evans

Moderately Bright, with Enthusiasm

VERSE

There's a new dance

sweep-ing the na-tion, you dance full of e-la-tion, do dance, let 'em all see your

stuff. Mis-ter, who can re-sist it? Sis-ter,

tod-dle and twist it, no one ev-er can get e-nough!

CHORUS

Give ___ 'em a thrill with ev-'ry ounce! Nev-er be coy,

nev-er be shy, give 'em that boom boom right in the eye, do that sug-ar ba-by bounce...

Lad-dy, dad-dy, don't ___ be a

fraid. Do that ___ sug-ar ba-by bounce,___ bounce a-round, bounce a-round!

Sugar Baby Bounce-7-3

just do that sug-ar ba-by bounce!___

DUET
Boom bam wig-gle your bot-tom, flip flop jig-gle your top,
Lad - dy, dad - dy, don't___ be a - fraid.

do - in' that sug-ar ba-by bounce!___ There's noth - in'
Do that___ sug-ar ba - by bounce,___ bounce a - round, bounce a - round!

Never be coy, nev-er be shy, give 'em that boom boom

Oh, ba-by nev - er___ ev - er___ drop it___

right in the eye! Come on, ba-by,___ don't say may-be to that

or for-sake it, just come on, ba-by,___ don't say may-be to that

sug - ar ba - by bounce! I said, "Bounce!"

sug - ar ba - by bounce! I said, "Bounce!"

Sugar Baby Bounce-7-7

From the Broadway Musical "Sugar Babies"

When You And I Were Young Maggie Blues

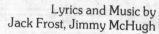

Lyrics and Music by
Jack Frost, Jimmy McHugh

CHORUS

From the Broadway Musical "Where's Charley?"

Once In Love With Amy

Lyrics and Music by
Frank Loesser

Slow and easy soft shoe

ONCE IN LOVE WITH A-MY, __ Al-ways in love with A-my. __

Ev-er and ev-er fas-cin-at-ed by 'er, Sets your heart a-fire __ to stay.

Once you're kissed by A-my, __ Tear up your list, it's A-my. __

Ply her with bon-bons, po-et-ry and flow-ers, Moon a mil-lion hours a-way. __ You

From the Broadway Musical "Wildcat"

Hey, Look Me Over

Lyrics and Music by
Carolyn Leigh, Cy Coleman

Interlude *(ad lib.)*

No - bod - y in the world was ev - er with - out a pray'r;

How can you win the world, if no - bod - y knows you're there.

Kid, when you need the crowd, the tick - ets are hard to sell;

Still you can lead the crowd, if you can get up and yell:

D. S. %

a tempo

From the Broadway Musical "Whoopee!"

Makin' Whoopee!

Lyrics and Music by
Gus Kahn, Walter Donaldson

THE BEST OF BROADWAY